The Little Monk Meditates...

The Little Monk Meditates...

Text and Illustrations by
John C. Huntington

New York Weatherhill Tokyo

First edition, 1995

Published by Weatherhill, Inc.
568 Broadway, Suite 705, New York, New York 10012

Protected by copyright under terms of the International Copyright Union; all rights reserved. Except for fair use in book reviews, no part of this book may be reproduced for any reason by any means, including any method of photographic reproduction, without permission of the publisher.

Printed in Hong Kong.

Library of Congress Cataloging-in-Publication Data:

Huntington, John C.
   The little monk meditates... / by John C. Huntington
   — Ist ed.
       p.   cm.   —(Meditation techniques ; 2)
   Contents: —2. Cognitive identity transfer in preliminary
Devayoga.
  ISBN 0-8348-0329-I
  I. Mediation—Buddhism 2. Buddhist art and symbolism.
I. Title.   II. Series.
BQ5612.H86   1995
294.3443—dc20   94-45802
                             CIP

Foreword

A Buddha is an enlightened being who works ceaselessly for the well-being of others without regard for any possible benefits for himself or herself. While all Buddhas have marvelous transcendent qualities, they are not "gods" in the Judaeo-Christian sense. Fundamentally, a Buddha is always a teacher (guru) of a method of spiritual release who, both by example and instruction, attempts to lead others along the path to salvation.

Vairocana Buddha (the Buddha of Infinite Luminosity) in this meditation is the eternal, adamantine, and primordial essence of all Buddhas. The so-called historical Buddha, known either as Gautama Buddha or Shakyamuni Buddha, is but one of a long line of mortal Buddhas who were realizations of that Buddha essence which is embodied in Vairocana.

According to the Buddhist teachings, one's true Buddha-nature resides almost dormant and totally unrecognized in the heart/mind of every sentient being. To awaken it from its dormancy and bring it into one's awareness, the individual must perform a series of conscious, deliberate actions. This effort cannot, indeed, must not, be one of ego gratification or self-aggrandizement, for such attitudes are inevitably roads to lower rebirth. The effort will only be effective if the true motivation is to enable the seeker to come to the aid of others.

Over the centuries, attempts to express the Buddha-nature have filled tens of thousands of volumes and produced millions of paintings, sculptures, ritual implements, stupas, and other works of architecture. Yet for most even a first glimpse of the potential for enlightenment remains difficult to attain. This small volume attempts to evoke a sense of that initial realization and may serve as a first step on the path that is the way of the Buddhas.

Aum Shanti Sarva—May There Be Universal Peace

The Little Monk Meditates...

*The Little Monk
begins to meditate
on Vairocana.*

*Sit comfortably in a place

you have just cleaned.

Then, with completely altruistic

intentions and without ego,

purify your mind.*

*The Little Monk
first visualizes
Vairocana.*

*Vairocana Buddha
embodies the totality
of the Buddhist teachings.*

The Little Monk visualizes Vairocana emanating all Buddhas.

Vairocana is the unity of pure Compassion and consummate Wisdom that is the full enlightenment of all Buddhas.

*The Little Monk
visualizes the Buddhas
expanding throughout
the universe.*

*All Buddhas

throughout the universe are

manifestly identical to and

are one with Vairocana.*

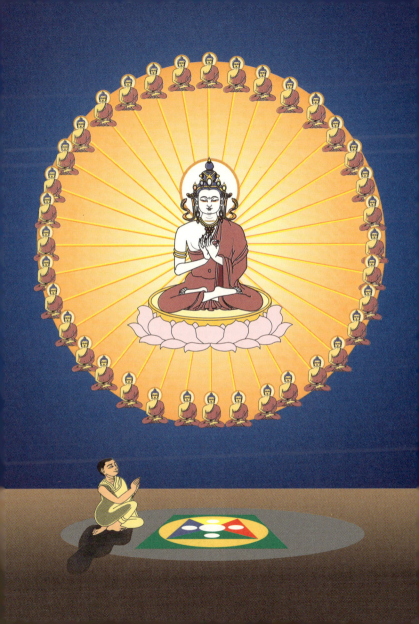

*The Little Monk
opens the channel of
rainbow light into
his heart/mind.*

Once recognized,

Vairocana Buddha must be

realized as the very core

of our heart/mind of being.

*The Little Monk
visualizes Vairocana
beginning to dissolve
into light.*

*Vairocana's true nature is
pure, brilliant white light
that illuminates
the totality of space.*

*The Little Monk
visualizes Vairocana
as brilliant light
without differentiation.*

*Vairocana can reveal his
transcendant form to those
who begin to perfect their
Wisdom and Compassion
toward others.*

*The Little Monk
absorbs the Vairocana
light into his
heart/mind rainbow.*

*The potential of their own

enlightenment resides

in the heart/mind

of all beings.*

*The Little Monk absorbs
the visualization
of Vairocana into his
heart/mind.*

One's own Vairocana nature

is realized by altruistic

compassionate actions

for the benefit of all beings.

*The Little Monk
understands that
he is the self
of Vairocana's being.*

*The preliminary goal
of all Buddhist practice is experiencing,
even just glimpsing, the Buddha within
and then developing one's own
will to seek enlightenment.*

*The Little Monk
dissolves into
Vairocana's
state of existence.*

*The Vairocana state of being
is more fully realized by
endlessly striving for the Wisdom
that enables the performance
of compassionate actions.*

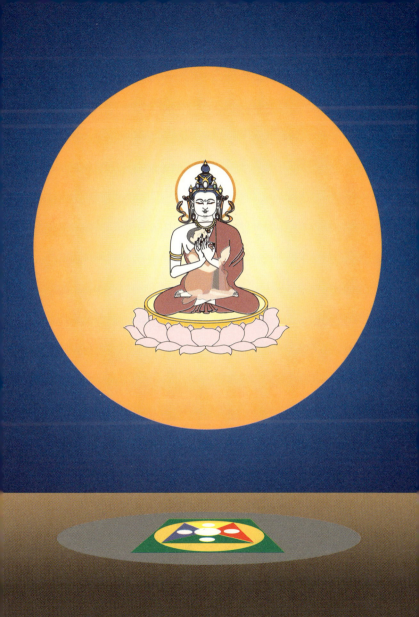

*The Little Monk
is identical
with Vairocana.*

Once Wisdom has been developed,

our lives are altruistically

devoted to the benefit of

others—

The "weathermark" identifies this book as a production of Weatherhill, Inc.,
publishers of fine books on Asia and the Pacific.
Editorial supervision: Jeffrey Hunter. Production supervision: Bill Rose.
Book and cover design: David Noble. Printing and binding: Oceanic Graphics
Press, Hong Kong. The typeface used is Centaur.